LIVING WITH
DIABETES

Jenny Bryan

Wayland

an imprint of Hodder Children's Books

Titles in the series

Living with Asthma

Living with Blindness

Living with Cerebral Palsy

Living with Deafness

Living with Diabetes

Living with Down's Syndrome

Living with Epilepsy

Living with Leukaemia

Series editor: Cath Senker
Book editor: Liz Harman
Cover design: Steve Wheele Design
Inside design: Peter Laws
Consultant: Nick Tapp, Acting Chief Executive, East Sussex Disability Association

First published in 1998 by Wayland Publishers Ltd

Reprinted in 2000 by Hodder Wayland, an imprint of Hodder Children's Books

British Library Cataloguing in Publication Data
Bryan, Jenny
    Living with Diabetes
    1. Diabetes – Juvenile literature
    I.Title II.Diabetes
    362.1'9'6462

ISBN 0 7502 2838 5

Printed and bound in Italy by G. Canale and C.S.p.A.

Picture acknowledgements
Hodder Wayland would like to thank: The British Diabetic Association
cover (top left), 7 (top), 20, 26, 27 (bottom), 29; Chapel Studios 12, 13, 23; Science
Photo Library/Simon Fraser 9 (top), Science Photo Library/St Bartholomew's Hospital
9 (bottom), Science Photo Library/Chris Priest & Mark Clarke 21, Science Photo
Library/Mark Clarke 22 (top), Science Photo Library/Russell D. Curtis 22 (bottom);
Tony Stone/Getty Images 28; Wayland Picture Library 7 (bottom), 8, 14, 15 (both),
27 (top).

All the other photographs were taken for Hodder Wayland by Angela Hampton.
Most of the people who are photographed in this book are models.
The illustration on page 6 is by Michael Courtney

Hodder Children's Books, a division of Hodder Headline Plc,
338 Euston Road, London NW1 3BH

This book has been produced in association with the
British Diabetic Association.

Contents

Meet Julie, Tim, Mr Hussain and Charlie

Julie has had diabetes for as long as she can remember. She needs injections of insulin twice a day. Her mother used to give them to her but now Julie does them herself. Sometimes she injects her leg, at other times she injects her arm or her stomach. She's very good at it now and it really doesn't hurt at all.

▽ Ian didn't know about diabetes until he met his friend Tim.

△ A timer on her computer reminds Julie to have her injections.

Ian was very worried when his friend, Tim, felt dizzy on the bus home from school. No one knew what to do. Ian knew that Tim had diabetes but didn't know that he needed a snack in the afternoon and had forgotten to eat it.

◁ Charlie loves sport, especially roller-blading, baseball and tennis.

Charlie and his sister, Mai, were born in Hong Kong but the family live in the USA now. Charlie seems to get lots of attention because he has diabetes. Mai can't understand what all the fuss is about because Charlie can do everything that other boys do.

△ Jemilla reminds her Grandpa to take his tablets every day.

Mr Hussain has had diabetes since he was 50 and it's given him other problems with his health. Sometimes his feet hurt and he finds it painful to walk. So his granddaughter, Jemilla, fetches things for him. Jemilla also goes to the hospital with her grandfather when he needs to see the doctor. She translates for him because he doesn't speak English very well.

What is diabetes?

We all need energy – not just to run about but all the time, even when we are asleep. We get our energy from food. People who have diabetes can't turn sugar from their food into energy.

If you have diabetes, your body does not have or cannot make the best use of a chemical called insulin. The body makes insulin in a gland called the pancreas, which lies across the back of the stomach. Insulin is needed to use the sugar in the blood for energy. It also controls the level of sugar in the blood.

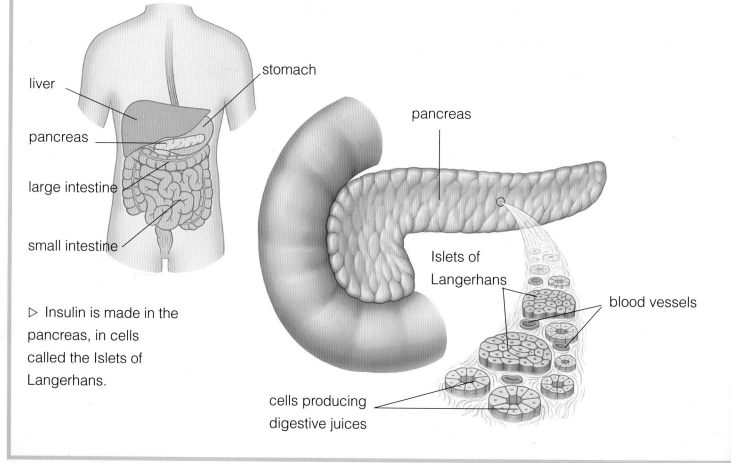

liver

stomach

pancreas

large intestine

small intestine

▷ Insulin is made in the pancreas, in cells called the Islets of Langerhans.

pancreas

Islets of Langerhans

blood vessels

cells producing digestive juices

There are two main types of diabetes. Julie, Tim and Charlie have the kind that is commonest in children – type 1 diabetes. When they were very young, their pancreases stopped making insulin. No one really knows why this happens. Without any insulin, they cannot make energy. Instead, all the sugar in their food stays in their blood or is passed out of the body in their urine.

△ Type 2 diabetes tends to start in older people, especially if they are overweight.

Mr Hussain has type 2 diabetes, which is more common than type 1. His pancreas can still make insulin but the rest of his body cannot use it properly. The result is the same as with type 1 diabetes – there is too much sugar in the blood.

Scientists believe that many people who cannot make or use insulin properly inherit the problem from their parents.

▷ Like hair colour and height, diabetes tends to run in families.

Treating diabetes

Without treatment, people with type 1 and type 2 diabetes feel very ill. They lose weight and become weak and tired because they cannot get any energy from their food. Before doctors found out how to treat the problem, people with diabetes eventually became unconscious and died.

Now, treatment is very effective. People who do not make any insulin, such as Julie, Tim and Charlie, can have insulin injections. Insulin always has to be injected. If you swallow insulin, it will be broken down in the stomach and intestine before it has a chance to work.

▷ Without treatment, people with diabetes feel very thirsty, drink lots of fluids and have to urinate often.

◁ A doctor doing a simple blood test to discover whether a patient has diabetes.

▽ A nurse showing a girl how to give herself an insulin injection in her thigh.

People with type 2 diabetes, like Mr Hussain, do not usually take insulin at first because their pancreas can still make it. Some people can control their sugar levels just by eating the right foods and losing weight. Many have to take tablets to control their sugar levels. People with type 2 diabetes usually have insulin injections only if other treatments do not work.

It is very important that people take their medicine every day. If they don't, they will feel ill and, when they are older, they may have problems with their eyes, their feet or their kidneys.

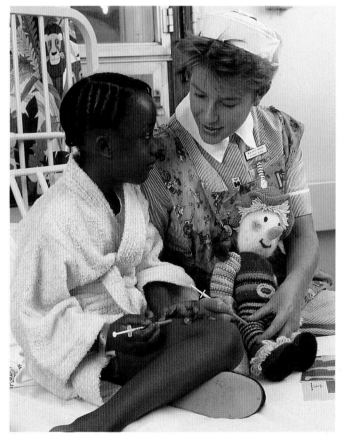

Julie's Day

Every morning, Julie has to get up in plenty of time to get ready for school. She needs to have her first insulin injection of the day about half an hour before breakfast. The insulin needs to be in her blood waiting to help her body to use the energy in her breakfast cereal.

People who have type 1 diabetes don't usually choose to give themselves an injection every time they eat something. It wouldn't be very nice to have lots of injections every day! Instead, Julie has two injections each day – one before breakfast and the second in the evening. Some people inject more often.

▽ Julie finds it less uncomfortable to give herself injections into a fatty part like her thigh.

△ When she has had her injection, Julie is ready for her meal.

Not a problem!

'Some people feel sorry for me because I have to give myself injections but I have got used to it now and I don't mind. At first, Mum or Dad used to help but now I do them on my own.'

△ Julie and her friends use up lots of energy during their PE lessons.

The insulin Julie has injected carries on working all day. This means that she needs to have all her meals at set times, as well as extra snacks between meals, so that the insulin has something to work on. If Julie forgets to have one snack in the morning and one in the afternoon, she may end up with too little sugar in her blood. This makes her feel shaky or dizzy, as Tim did on the bus. Julie may also have something extra to eat before a PE lesson, when she needs extra energy.

Food and diabetes

Take a look at the meal in the picture below. Think about what is in each dish. Which items do you think contain a lot of sugar? Which of these foods do you think someone with diabetes can eat?

The picture on the right shows the sort of meal that a person with diabetes might eat. It is surprisingly similar to the first picture. A person with diabetes could eat all the foods shown in the first picture. The main difference is that they should eat smaller portions of some foods and larger amounts of others.

◁ This meal is quite high in fat and sugar.

◁ Although this is very similar to the meal in the picture opposite, it contains less fat and sugar.

There is no reason why someone with diabetes should not eat foods that contain sugar or fat, such as biscuits, crisps or sweets. But they should try to eat less of these foods and choose low-fat, low-sugar snacks instead. People with diabetes can eat chips but mostly they should eat baked or boiled potatoes instead. Fizzy drinks are OK too, but they should choose low-sugar or sugar-free brands.

People with diabetes need to control their weight and may also have heart problems. A diet that is high in fat can make you put on weight and can be bad for your heart. If you have diabetes, you need to make sure that you do not eat too much fat.

A healthy diet

It is important that everyone should eat a healthy, balanced diet. Most people eat too much fat and sugar. Instead of sugary, fatty snacks, it is better to fill up on starchy foods like bread, pasta and potatoes. Fruit is a healthy snack to eat between meals and has plenty of fibre to help digestion. Baked beans, peas and lentils also contain lots of fibre.

Look again at the picture on page 13. You will see that a healthy diet for a person with diabetes is very similar to the diet that everyone should try to eat in order to stay healthy. As you can see, this doesn't mean you have to cut out all your favourite things.

▷ These foods are high in starch and fibre, but low in sugar and fat.

◁ For a healthy diet, we should aim to eat at least five helpings of fruit and vegetables every day.

▽ If you read labels, you can find out which foods are best for a healthy diet.

It is getting easier to find out how much fat, protein, sugar, vitamins and minerals are in our food. Most food labels now show this sort of information, which helps us all to plan a healthy diet.

Mr Hussain wants to fast

The Hussains are Muslims. Jemilla is going to the hospital with her grandfather to talk to the nurse about fasting during Ramadan. Ramadan is the ninth month in the Muslim calendar and, for about a month, Muslim adults fast between sunrise and sunset. During that time, they do not eat or drink. Instead, they eat two large meals a day, one just before sunrise and the other soon after sunset. The meals often contain a lot of fat and sugar to give people energy for the long fast.

Fasting is difficult for people with diabetes because they need to eat at regular times, as well as having snacks between meals.

▷ The nurse advised Mr Hussain not to eat too many sweet things during the two meals he has on each day of Ramadan.

A healthier diet

△ When he fasted last year, Mr Hussain felt unwell. This year, he knows how to make sure he doesn't feel ill.

'Grandad used to eat rich curries, but when he found he had diabetes, the doctor advised him to eat less fat. Now, Mum cooks meals using leaner meat, such as chicken, and just a little vegetable oil instead of animal fat. So the whole family has a healthier diet!'

The nurse advised Mr Hussain to change the dose and timing of his tablets while he fasts. It is difficult to adapt insulin treatment to fasting. Sometimes it is possible to change the dose. No one with diabetes should fast without talking to their doctor and working out how to avoid problems.

Learning about diabetes

After Tim had a dizzy spell on the bus one day, his friends wanted to learn more about diabetes. Tim's teacher asked the diabetes nurse from the hospital to come and talk to the class.

The nurse explained why Tim had felt dizzy on the bus. There wasn't enough sugar in his blood because he had forgotten to have a quick snack before he played football. The name for this is hypoglycaemia. People with diabetes who feel dizzy or shaky because they have hypoglycaemia sometimes say they have had a 'hypo'.

▽ The nurse drew some pictures to show how the pancreas works.

I'm not different!

'At first, I didn't want people to know I've got diabetes. I don't want them to treat me as if I'm different – I don't feel different! I was nervous when the nurse came to talk to the class, but I think my friends understand more about diabetes now.'

▷ The nurse showed the class the sugar tablets that Tim carries in case he feels dizzy.

The class talked about the kinds of snack that Tim should eat. He needs something like a biscuit to give the insulin something to work on.

Tim keeps a packet of sugar tablets with him. If he has a 'hypo', the tablets will quickly raise his blood-sugar level.

It is very unusual for someone with diabetes to become unconscious because they have too little sugar in their blood. Normally, they just feel dizzy, shaky, sweaty or tired, like Tim. But the nurse explained to the class that if someone diabetes collapses, they should get help straight away by telling an adult or telephoning for an ambulance.

◁ Ian helps Tim by reminding him to eat his snacks.

Health check

People with diabetes can't just take their medicine and hope it will keep their blood sugar under control. They have to be sure, so once or twice a day they do a special test.

Everyone with type 1 diabetes and some people with type 2 diabetes test a drop of their blood. They prick their finger and put the blood on a plastic strip. Some strips fit into a small, hand-held machine, which shows how much sugar is in the blood. Other strips change colour to show blood-sugar level.

A test before breakfast and one before the evening meal show how well the insulin is working. But sometimes people with diabetes need to measure their blood-sugar level during the day.

◁ This girl is checking her blood-sugar level by doing a simple blood test.

If there is too much or too little sugar in their blood, their doctor or nurse can show them how to change the amount of insulin or tablets they take. They may also have to think more carefully about what they eat.

People with type 2 diabetes can check how well their medicines are working by testing the amount of sugar in their urine. All they have to do is dip a plastic strip in a small sample of urine and see what colour it turns.

△ This boy will soon feel in control of his diabetes, once his doctor has explained how to do tests.

Gadgets and gizmos

Injecting insulin gets easier all the time. Some people use an ordinary syringe but many use a syringe that looks like a small pen. They insert a tiny container of insulin and, when they press the blunt end of the pen, it injects insulin through the skin. It is simple to use and looks like a normal pen.

Instead of injecting themselves with a syringe, a few people choose to wear a small device that they can set to inject insulin at certain times. They wear the device all the time. It has a small control box attached to a needle which is in the person's skin.

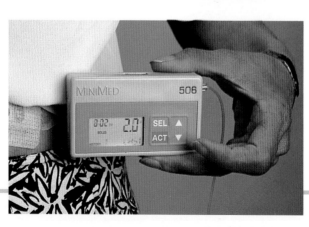

▷ A small insulin pump like this gives injections at the times set by the person wearing it.

△ Some people prefer to use an insulin pen like this because it is easier to use than a syringe.

At least once a year, people with diabetes should have a health check. This often includes blood tests and checks on their eyes, nerves and kidneys. There are usually special doctors and nurses who are used to treating diabetes and know all about it. They can help to sort out any problems.

▽ People with diabetes make sure they stay healthy by having regular medical check-ups.

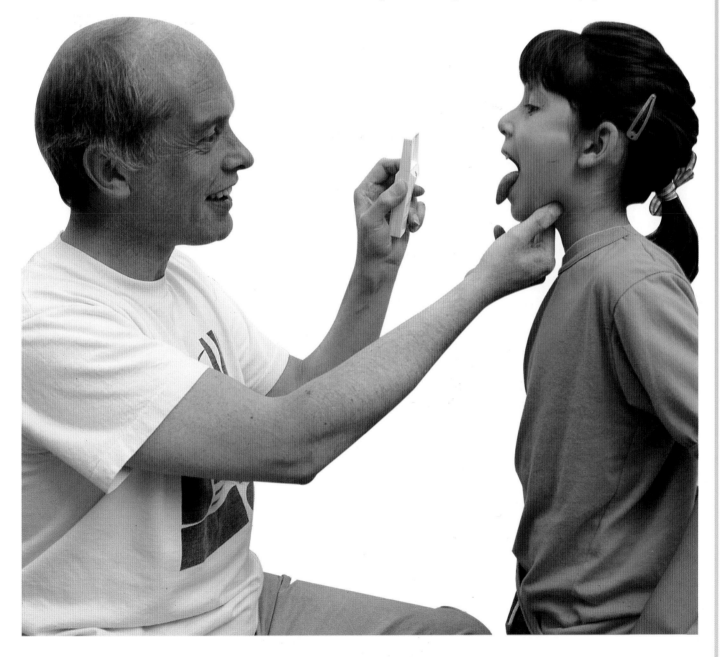

A family matter

Mai was fed up. Just when she needed her Dad to help her with her homework, he was helping Charlie to test his blood for sugar.

'It's always the same,' grumbled Mai. 'Charlie gets all the attention and nobody cares about me!'

'You know that's not true,' said her father. 'I came to watch you in the school play yesterday instead of going to Charlie's baseball game.'

Dad sat down with Mai and Charlie. Both children know a lot about diabetes already. They understand what causes it and why Charlie needs insulin injections. Mai tries not to eat sweets in front of Charlie because she knows he cannot have them as often as she can.

△ Dad wanted to see the result of Charlie's blood test but Mai was feeling left out.

'Sometimes, Charlie's diabetes has to come first,' said Dad. 'He needs to test his blood every day and have his injections on time, otherwise he might be ill.'

'I know,' said Mai. 'But it always seems to be when I need you too.' Dad laughed. 'It only takes a few minutes to help Charlie and there's plenty of time to help you too.'

△ Mai and Charlie both felt better after their talk with Dad.

'I do most of my injections and tests on my own now, so I won't need so much help in future,' said Charlie.

'That's right, and then we can both help Mai with her homework,' said Dad.

Mai pulled a face and said, 'If Charlie tries to help, I'm sure to get it all wrong!'

Will diabetes ever go away?

Scientists are trying to find out more about diabetes. They want to improve treatment so that people don't develop problems with their eyes, feet, heart, kidneys and nerves. Doctors are studying the way people can inherit diabetes from their parents. They hope to find a way to prevent both types of diabetes. Another aim is to find a way to give people with diabetes a new pancreas. Doctors can transplant organs like the kidney and heart but transplanting a pancreas is more difficult.

▽ Scientists are trying to find out how diabetes is passed on from parents to children.

It may be many years before scientists find a way to prevent diabetes. But there are lots of things you can do to protect yourself from getting type 2 diabetes when you are older.

▷ Make exercise a part of your life and stay fit.

▽ Because they can develop foot problems, people with diabetes need to look after their feet.

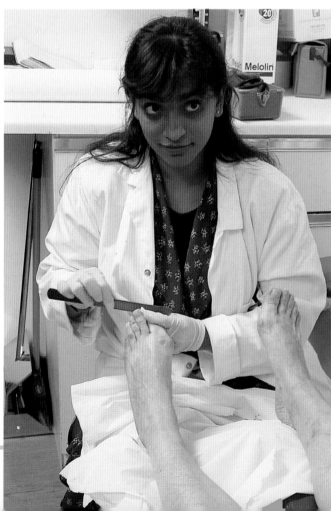

Adults are more likely to get diabetes if they are overweight. By eating a healthy diet and taking plenty of exercise now, you can help to make sure that you will be healthier later in life.

Nobody wants to have diabetes. But you've seen that Julie, Tim, Charlie and Mr Hussain all lead normal, active lives. They don't let their diabetes get in the way. You don't need to feel sorry for people with diabetes or to keep away from them.

Getting help

People who have diabetes get to know the doctors and nurses who look after them. They usually need most help when they first discover that they have diabetes. It takes a while to get used to checking your blood sugar, taking your insulin or other medicine, and planning a healthy diet.

In most countries, there are organizations specially for people with diabetes. They bring together groups of people with diabetes and their families. It is good to talk to other people who have diabetes. They may have had similar problems and experiences and might have some useful ideas about how to cope.

△ A group of people with type 2 diabetes meet to talk and give each other support.

The British Diabetic Association (BDA) gives help and support to people with diabetes in the UK. You can contact the BDA at 10 Queen Anne Street, London W1M 0BD. The BDA has groups all over the country – there will be one near you. Some meet to talk about diabetes. They may even organize trips and outings.

▷ These young people are on an activity holiday organized by a support group for people with diabetes.

Children with diabetes can go on all the usual family holidays and school trips that other children enjoy. But sometimes, it is good for them to meet others on a holiday where everyone has diabetes, to share experiences and gain confidence. Groups like the BDA organize activity holidays to help children to meet and have a good time.

The more you know about diabetes and how to look after it, the less scary it is.

Glossary

Blood A liquid which flows all around the body, carrying oxygen and protein, fat and sugar from our food.

Cell All living things are made up of millions of tiny parts, called cells. Groups of millions of cells form organs like the pancreas.

Digestion The process by which the body breaks down food and turns it into energy and waste products.

Dose A carefully worked-out amount of a drug.

Fast To go without food (and sometimes drink).

Fat Part of our food which gives us energy. Eating too much fat can make you overweight and can damage your heart.

Fibre A part of food that helps to keep the intestine healthy.

Gland A small part of the body which produces chemicals, such as insulin.

Hypoglycaemia Lower than normal levels of sugar in the blood.

Inherit To be born with a physical problem or feature that has been passed on from the body of a parent.

Insulin A chemical made by the pancreas which controls sugar levels in the body.

Intestine A long tube which is part of the system that digests food.

Kidney An organ in the lower part of the body which processes body waste and produces urine.

Mineral A natural substance found in some foods, which is needed to keep the body healthy.

Nerve A thin fibre which passes messages around the body.

Pancreas The gland which makes insulin and other chemicals needed for digestion.

Protein An important part of our food which is needed for growth and to repair damaged parts of the body.

Ramadan A period of fasting carried out by Muslim adults. It is one of the most important requirements of the Islamic religion.

Syringe A small plastic or glass tube with a needle at one end. A syringe is used to inject substances into the body through the skin.

Transplant To move a healthy organ from one body to another body, to replace an organ that no longer works properly.

Urine A waste fluid produced by the kidneys.

Vitamin A natural substance found in some foods, which is needed to keep the body healthy.

Further information

Diabetes by Marjorie Little (Chelsea House, 1991)

Diabetes by Alvin Silverstein (Enslow Publishers, 1994)

Diabetes and Charlie Chocolate by Julie Alfrey (Children's Meducational Books, 1994)

Your local doctor's surgery or hospital will be able to provide you with information about diabetes and its treatment.

Further leaflets, videos, magazines and books can be obtained from the BDA at the address mentioned on page 29.

There are many Internet sites about diabetes. The following are designed for children:

- http://www.castleweb.com/diabetes.
  Produced by Children with Diabetes, this site gives access to information, groups and penpals.

- http://www.diabetes.com/site.
  The American Diabetes Association web site. Look for Kool Kids.

- http://www.diabetes.org.uk.
  The British Diabetic Association web site, which has information for children, adults, families and friends.

- http://www.geocities.com/HotSprings/6935/index.html.
  A site for children who want to learn about diabetes.

- http://www.thehumanelement.com/courage/.
  Cartoons about Courage, the superhero who has diabetes.

Index

Numbers in **bold** refer to pictures.